HSE
Health & Safety
Executive

HEALTH RISK MANAGEMENT

A practical guide for managers in small and medium-sized enterprises

HSE BOOKS

First published 1995

Reprinted 1996, 1999, 2000 (with amendments)

HSG137

ISBN 0 7176 0905 7

This guidance is issued by the Health and Safety Executive. Following the guidance is not compulsory and you are free to take other action. But if you do follow the guidance you will normally be doing enough to comply with the law. Health and safety inspectors seek to secure compliance with the law and may refer to this guidance as illustrating good practice.

FOREWORD

The Health and Safety Commission and Executive are convinced that good health and safety management is the key to achieving real improvements in all aspects of health and safety at work, and that this should lead to greater efficiency and cost savings. Improving health and safety management continues to be one of our priority tasks. I believe that this guide will help small and medium sized employers in particular to recognise that managing work-related health risks need not be difficult, and that they can do it successfully. The results will benefit both individual employees and the company as a whole.

Frank J Davies CBE, OStJ
Chairman, Health and Safety Commission

CONTENTS

INTRODUCTION

1   This booklet has been prepared to help the owners and managers of small and medium sized enterprises to control health risks arising from work. It is based on information and experience gained by HSE, and actual case studies are used to illustrate particular points. Management needs to be competent to deal effectively with occupational health risks.

2   Each year more people become ill as a result of their work than are killed or injured in industrial accidents (Box 1). While most diseases caused by work do not kill, they can involve years of pain, suffering and discomfort for those affected. This might include musculo-skeletal problems, respiratory disease, dermatitis and noise induced hearing loss.

Box 1

Approximately 1 million people suffer a workplace injury each year.
2 million people suffer ill health caused or made worse by work.
Altogether 30 million working days a year are lost due to workplace injuries and ill health.

3   As a manager you will be concerned if your employees' health is affected by their work. Management skills can be applied to preventing ill health as part of running a business. The link between the workplace cause and later ill health is not always obvious. This booklet provides a framework and some examples to help you to improve the control of health risks in your workplace.

Table 1 **Hazards to health**

Hazardous chemicals – if inhaled can cause asthma, bronchitis or cancer; if swallowed can cause poisoning; if spilt onto the skin or splashed into the eyes can cause dermatitis or severe irritation.

Sprains, strains and pains – can be caused by manual lifting of heavy loads. Upper limb disorders (ULDs), so called repetitive strain injury (RSI), can happen if the workstation is poorly designed so that people have to adopt awkward body positions. ULDs can also occur as a result of repetitive or fast movements, poor posture and high forces.

Noise – noise levels which are too high (eg having to shout to be heard) can lead to deafness or conditions such as tinnitus (ringing in the ears).

Vibration – too much vibration, eg from continual use of powered hand tools, can lead to debilitating diseases such as vibration white finger.

Ionising radiation – eg exposure to X-rays, can cause burns, sickness and cancer. Non-ionising radiation such as infra-red and ultra-violet radiation and lasers can all damage the eyes and skin. Microwaves can cause excessive heating of exposed parts of the body.

Extremes of temperature, pressure and humidity – can affect people's ability to work safely and can cause harmful changes within their bodies, such as heat stress and 'the bends' (pressure).

Hazardous micro-organisms – eg bacteria, if inhaled, swallowed, accidentally injected into the skin, splashed into the eyes or allowed to contaminate skin cuts can cause disease, allergy or toxic effects. While the majority of micro-organisms are harmless some can lead to potentially fatal conditions such as legionnaires' disease and Weil's disease.

Stress – can affect all employees, not just managers. It is often behind a lot of sickness absences. It can contribute to coronary heart disease and illness caused by high blood pressure.

4   Many employers wait for a health problem to arise before doing something about it, but this can result in:

- employees being made ill or even killed,

- lost time;

- unplanned changes to the work;

- retraining;

- bad publicity;

- investigation by health and safety inspectors;

- employees taking early retirement, employees with a reduced quality of life;

- court fines and legal fees;

- compensation claims;

- increased insurance premiums.

What the law requires

5   There are legal duties on employers to prevent ill health which can be caused by work. The two main pieces of law are the Health and Safety at Work etc Act 1974 (HSW Act) and the Management of Health and Safety at Work Regulations 1992 (MHSW Regulations) as amended.

6   Under the HSW Act, employers have to ensure so far as is reasonably practicable the health and safety of employees and others who may be affected by their work. The Act applies to all work activities and premises. Employers are required to provide suitable plant and systems of work, to train, instruct, inform and supervise employees so that their health at work is not affected. Employees have responsibilities under the HSW Act not to endanger themselves or others.

7   The MHSW Regulations build on the HSW Act and include duties to assess risks and make arrangements for health and safety by effective:

- planning;

- organisation;

- control;

- monitoring and review.

HSC's Approved Code of Practice on the MHSW Regulations gives guidance on what is meant by these terms. This guide gives more detail, particularly in relation to health risks.

8   The MHSW Regulations also contain duties for health surveillance which is about looking for early signs of ill health caused by hazards at work. In addition all employers are required to appoint a competent person to assist in complying with health and safety legal requirements and in the design and use of protective measures. The person appointed to assist could be one of your managers who has been properly trained to do this, although if the risks are complicated, or their management involves special knowledge, you may need to involve people from outside your business (see Table 2, p 38).

9   In addition there are several laws (Box 2) that relate to specific risks to health at work, such as lead, asbestos, chemicals and noise, and some that relate to particular industries (Box 3). Look at them to find out what you must do.

Box 2   Examples of health and safety legal requirements for specific health risks at work

Control of Substances Hazardous to Health (COSHH) Regulations 1999
Control of Lead at Work Regulations 1998
Ionising Radiations Regulations 1985
Control of Asbestos at Work Regulations 1987
Noise at Work Regulations 1989
The Manual Handling Operations Regulations 1992
The Health and Safety (Display Screen Equipment) Regulations 1992

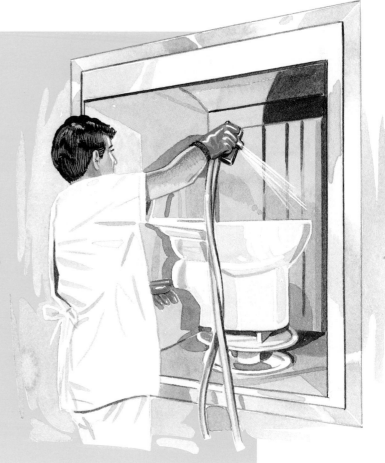

Box 3

A company employing 250 people in the manufacture of
bathroom fittings described the health and safety
legislation relating to their industry as providing 'a
framework for action'. The legislation pointed to those
risks they should give priority to and how to take steps to
manage the risks.

Being a traditional industry they were able to draw on a
range of existing specific guidance and established
industry practice.

What is health risk management?

10   Health risk management is about identifying and controlling health risks before they can cause problems and lead to the losses described in paragraph 4. To do this you need to:

- find out if you have a problem;

- decide what to do based on what you have found out;

- act and put the decisions into practice;

- check that the action has made the intended improvements.

This is what good health risk management is all about.

11   For this approach to work there needs to be commitment at the top of your organisation to achieving better health risk management. This should be expressed in a clear policy for health and safety which influences all your activities in a practical way. It should be clear about who is responsible for what, and the arrangements for identifying hazards, assessing risks and controlling them. Managers need to demonstrate their commitment to other members of the workforce and be the driving force behind making improvements. If *you* are not motivated neither will be the rest of the workforce. As a manager you are the key to what does or doesn't happen to improve health at work.

Box 4

'In a survey carried out of small companies who had a good control of health risks the one common factor identified was the commitment shown by top management.'
Quote from HSE inspector.

12   Good health risk management is also about teamwork. Talk to the workforce and involve them in sorting out problems and encourage early reporting. Use the knowledge and skills within your company; ask employees, their representatives, and members of the health and safety committee for their views and ideas. Tell the workforce about any changes in face to face talks, via posters and company leaflets. Remember that employees may need to be retrained following any changes, and safety representatives either appointed under the Safety Representatives and Safety Committees Regulations 1977 or the Health and Safety (Consultation with Employees) Regulations 1996 will need to be consulted in advance.

STAGE 1 FINDING OUT IF YOU HAVE A PROBLEM

Look for the hazards. 'Hazard' is anything that can cause harm (see Table 1).

13   The starting point in managing health risks is finding the hazards in your workplace, and there may be a wide range. Some hazards to health are not as immediately obvious as others. For example some substances give off invisible vapours and dusts, large quantities of which may be produced during handling activities.

To pinpoint hazards:

• walk around the workplace – take a fresh look at the way employees work, look at what they work with, look at what is already done to protect their health (Box 6 gives an example of how to do this);

• talk to employees – ask them if their work affects their health;

• get advice from suppliers of equipment, chemicals and other materials used at work (Box 5);

• read safety data sheets, manufacturers' and suppliers' guidance.

Remember, radiation and micro-organisms cannot be detected just by looking.

Box 5

Suppliers of hazardous substances are required to provide information to users which includes:
- safety data sheets;
- proper labelling designed to make hazards and necessary controls clear.

Some suppliers may also provide:
- training in the use of their products;
- workplace surveys on exposure to health hazards.

A fee may be charged for training and surveys, so ask your suppliers what help they can give you. For further information about this see Chemicals (Hazard Information and Packaging for Supply) (Amendment) Regulations 1997 known as CHIP.

Suppliers fo work equipment are also required to provide users with hazard data including:
- noise and vibration emissions;
- advice on safe use.

Box 6   Manual handling

As you walk around the workplace, look out for the
following activities:
- strenuous pulling or pushing;
- whether more than one person is required for
  the task;
- over-reaching;
- repetitive handling;
- reaching above shoulder height;
- getting into awkward postures;
- lifting heavy or awkward loads;
- carrying for long distances;
- lifting in awkward places.

Looking for these activities will help you
decide if you have manual handling problems
in the workplace.

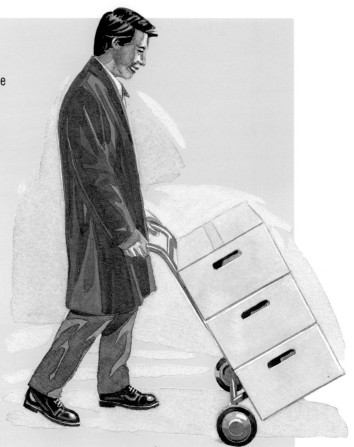

Provision of a simple manual handling aid
can eliminate the need to carry loads.

14   Changes to the law or new guidance can be a spur to tackling
long standing problems (Box 7).

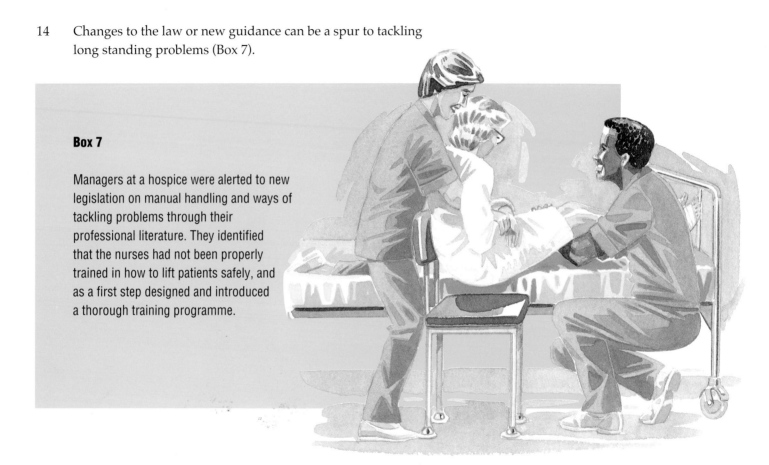

Box 7

Managers at a hospice were alerted to new
legislation on manual handling and ways of
tackling problems through their
professional literature. They identified
that the nurses had not been properly
trained in how to lift patients safely, and
as a first step designed and introduced
a thorough training programme.

15   If, for example, you handle a lot of chemicals, do not assume that your hazards to health will be associated only with chemicals. Find out whether there are other health hazards at your workplace such as noise from the process and manual handling problems in moving bulk chemical materials. At the back of this booklet is a list of other HSE guidance to help you tackle particular risks.

Lifestyle and work

16   Some health problems can be caused both at work and at home. Handling chemicals in the workplace can cause dermatitis, as can washing powder used at home. Lifting heavy loads at work can cause back injury, as can, for example, moving furniture at home and leisure activities. Some existing health conditions can be made worse by work; a heavy smoker is more likely to suffer breathing problems following exposure to chemicals at work.

17   Be aware of the overlaps between work and non-work health risks. Legally, as an employer you need to tackle only work-related risks but many companies do not distinguish between the two. They deal with health risks at work and also promote the need for employees to look after their health by, for example, giving advice on smoking and drinking, diet, and exercise. This is one company's reason: 'If someone does not turn up for work because of a bad back caused by work here or in their garden, the result for us is the same – no work'.

CHECKLIST

HAZARDS

☐ Have you looked at how work is carried out in your workplace?

☐ Have you found which hazards exist?

☐ Have you looked at available information, eg labels, suppliers' safety data sheets?

☐ Have you found out what your employees and their safety representatives think about the effect of work on their health?

☐ Have you considered who can help you?

DECIDING WHAT TO DO

18   Having found out what health hazards are present in your workplace you need now to decide what needs to be done so that your employees' health is not harmed. It may be that what you already do is enough but you cannot decide this properly until you have gone through the following steps.

Who might be harmed?

19   First, you need to identify who may be at risk. Think about those workers, for example, who handle chemicals, operate noisy machines or who have to lift heavy or awkward loads manually. Don't forget the risks to cleaners, maintenance and part-time workers. Could other people be harmed by what goes on in your place of work, for instance sales representatives, suppliers, customers and members of the public?

How big are the risks?

20   The next step is to decide how big are the risks to health in your workplace. 'Risk' is the chance or likelihood of someone being harmed by a hazard. For example, paints containing isocyanates are a hazard to health. Breathing in isocyanates can cause asthma. The health risk is the chance that someone's lungs will be damaged. Whether this happens will depend upon:

- the amount of isocyanate in the air;

- how often the job is done. Is it all day every day or once or twice a year?

- the work method – how the paint is used, eg if it is sprayed the risk will be greater than if brushed on;

- the number of people that could be affected – is just one person working with the paint or many? Could their work affect others?

- what could go wrong?

- are the precautions (exhaust ventilation, personal protective equipment) already taken sufficient? How do they compare with good practice and HSE or 'trade' guidance?

21   Answering these sorts of question is what is meant by risk assessment. Further guidance can be found in the free HSE leaflet *Five Steps to Risk Assessment*. It is useful to write down the results of risk assessments as you may need to look at them again. You are required to record 'significant findings' if you have five or more employees.

22   Remember also to review your risk assessment when the work changes and new materials are handled. It is easier to review it if it is written down.

Box 8   Summary of risk assessment steps

- Look for the hazards; decide who might be harmed and how;
- decide whether existing precautions are adequate or more should be done;
- record your findings;
- review your assessment.

23   Risk assessment will help you to decide which health risks should be given priority, for example if a large number of employees could be affected or if there is a risk of a serious disease. The aim is to identify what steps need to be taken to control or reduce risk. Many companies mistakenly think that risk assessment is an end in itself. The purpose is to help you decide whether what you already do to control health risks is enough or whether you need to do more (Box 9).

24   Records of accidents, ill health and sickness absence help you identify health risk effects and decide how serious they are. Look for trends - does the same problem keep cropping up? Is it

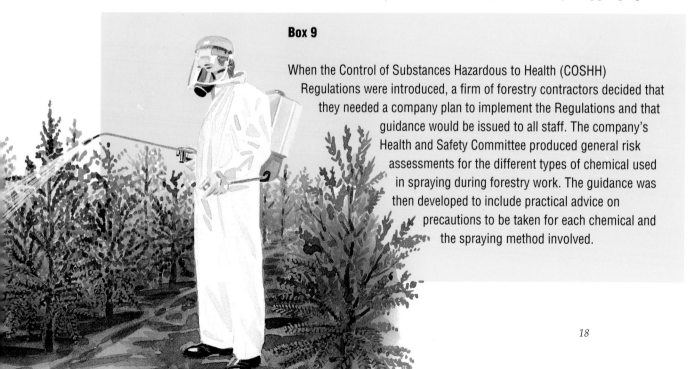

Box 9

When the Control of Substances Hazardous to Health (COSHH) Regulations were introduced, a firm of forestry contractors decided that they needed a company plan to implement the Regulations and that guidance would be issued to all staff. The company's Health and Safety Committee produced general risk assessments for the different types of chemical used in spraying during forestry work. The guidance was then developed to include practical advice on precautions to be taken for each chemical and the spraying method involved.

Box 10 Lost time accidents

Condition	Cause
Strained small of back	Twisted himself lifting pipes
Strained muscle right leg	Pulling ... hose into crate
Strained back muscle	Lifting ...
Strained shoulder and knee	Slipped
Pulled muscle top of leg	Overstretching
Strained back	Stepping onto platform

always associated with the same process? Is more than one person affected? Find out what is really causing someone to be off work. One company realised it had health problems at work because of the number of people leaving early to visit their GP.

25   In one factory (Box 10), the lost time accidents involving sprains and strains were recorded in one month. Each incident resulted in someone being off work. If this is a typical month there will be 36 incidents of people being off work with strains and sprains each year. Employees were off for 3 days on average which means 108 days of work are lost each year. Think of the cost involved to the company. This accident information confirmed that there were a number of handling problems at this workplace. They could be avoided by training or changing the work process to avoid twisting, overstretching and heavy lifting, eg by providing lifting devices.

What if a worker is ill?

26   Suppose an employee is off work for several days. Then a note from his/her GP confirms that the employee is suffering from dermatitis to the hands and wrists and is likely to be off work for several weeks. What do you do about this? An investigation will help you decide how to prevent it happening again (Box 11).

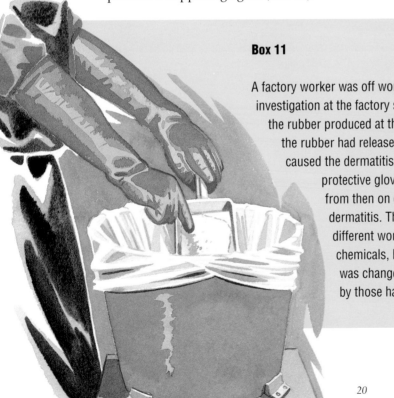

Box 11

A factory worker was off work. His GP had diagnosed dermatitis. An investigation at the factory showed that he used a chemical solvent with the rubber produced at the factory. A reaction between the solvent and the rubber had released a substance which was thought to have caused the dermatitis. The worker had not been wearing the protective gloves provided, and had become sensitised so that from then on exposure to the compound could lead to further dermatitis. The employee was retrained and assigned to different work. The company thought about using safer chemicals, but this was not possible. The work procedure was changed so that protective gloves were always worn by those handling solvent and rubber.

27   You need to find out whether an employee's ill health could have been caused or made worse by work. Ask these questions:

- What work has the employee been doing and how long for?

- Does the employee work with harmful materials or in such a way that his/her health could become affected?

- When did signs of ill health occur?

- What is the opinion of his/her GP and any occupational health advisers?

- Have the risks of the work activity been assessed?

- Does the risk assessment indicate that precautions are needed?

- Is the employee trained both for the job and in the use of any equipment used to control risk?

- Is protective clothing provided and used for the work?

- Could activities outside of work have caused ill health?

Box 12 Health surveillance

Following an assessment of the risk to employees' health due to hand arm vibration, a foundry decided the following actions were needed:
- firstly, it sought to eliminate, as far as possible, the need for fettling, by introducing modifications to casting design;
- secondly, it sought to reduce harmful vibration from tools and machines by retrofitting anti-vibration mountings and by assuring future purchases of tools had lower levels of harmful vibration;
- thirdly, a system of *health surveillance* was adopted in line with the recommendations of *Hand-arm vibration,* and a pre-employment medical assessment was instituted.

Although several employees in the company's long-established workforce were identified with early symptoms of vibration white finger, it was decided that there was no need for their relocation at this stage. The results from the ongoing health surveillance would give early warning of the progression of symptoms, or any new cases and redeployment to other work would then be considered. Additionally, the results would give feedback as to the effectiveness of the control measures taken.

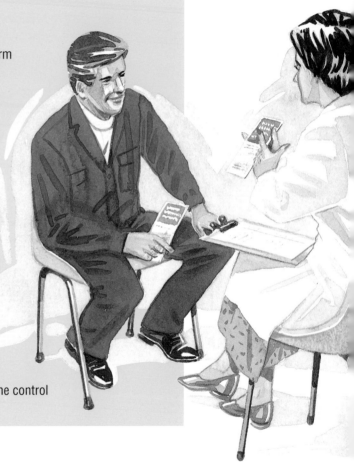

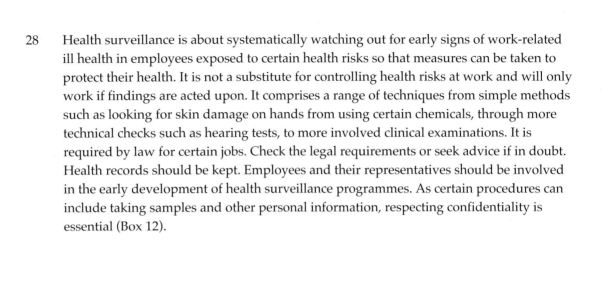

28   Health surveillance is about systematically watching out for early signs of work-related ill health in employees exposed to certain health risks so that measures can be taken to protect their health. It is not a substitute for controlling health risks at work and will only work if findings are acted upon. It comprises a range of techniques from simple methods such as looking for skin damage on hands from using certain chemicals, through more technical checks such as hearing tests, to more involved clinical examinations. It is required by law for certain jobs. Check the legal requirements or seek advice if in doubt. Health records should be kept. Employees and their representatives should be involved in the early development of health surveillance programmes. As certain procedures can include taking samples and other personal information, respecting confidentiality is essential (Box 12).

CHECKLIST

ACTION

☐ Have you identified and assessed all the risks to health in your workplace?

☐ Do the risk assessments cover all work procedures where there may be a health risk?

☐ Have the risk assessments identified all employees who may be at risk?

☐ Have you used the risk assessments to help decide what practical steps should be taken to manage risks to health?

☐ Do you find out the causes of work-related ill health and use the findings to prevent it happening again?

STAGE 3 TAKING ACTION

29   If you decide that improvements are needed, then act on your decisions. Start by seeing whether you can get rid of whatever is causing the health risks (Boxes 13 and 14).

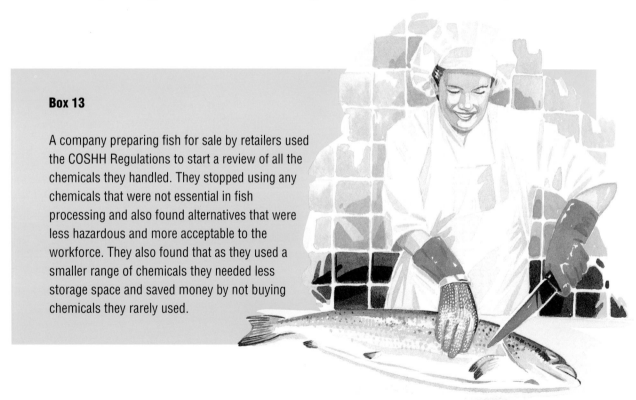

Box 13

A company preparing fish for sale by retailers used the COSHH Regulations to start a review of all the chemicals they handled. They stopped using any chemicals that were not essential in fish processing and also found alternatives that were less hazardous and more acceptable to the workforce. They also found that as they used a smaller range of chemicals they needed less storage space and saved money by not buying chemicals they rarely used.

Box 14

A rubber factory was aware of the risks associated with handling carbon black in rubber processing: also as it is usually supplied as a fine powder it made the workplace very dirty. Managers decided that they would stop handling carbon black and buy in rubber pre-mixed with carbon black. The benefits were:
- a hazardous material was no longer handled;
- a shorter process time;
- a cleaner workplace;
- less time spent cleaning up.

30   If you cannot do this the next step is to control the risks and so reduce the chance of the health of employees being affected. For example exposure to chemicals can be controlled by automated handling, enclosing the process or local exhaust ventilation.

31   The risk from heavy lifting can be removed by the use of lifting aids. Nurses in hospitals, for example, use patient-lifting aids. Exposure to noise levels can be reduced by enclosing noisy machines and equipment with noiseproof enclosures. Problems associated with repetitive manual work can be solved by redesigning or organising the work differently (Box 15).

Box 15   Redesign of work process or station

An employee's job was to answer telephone enquiries and check customer details by using a computer terminal. The employee complained of pain in her left shoulder, left arm, neck and back. Observation of the employee's method of work showed that the work involved continual reaching across the body due to the positions of the telephone and computer keyboard. Keyboard operations were carried out while the telephone receiver was cradled between the neck and left shoulder to free both hands. The computer screen was positioned to the right of the employee and as it could not be raised properly this added to the poor neck posture. The employee did not have a comfortable sitting position as her chair was not adjustable and a footrest had not been provided.

These changes were made:
- the screen was placed directly in front of the employee, it was also raised so that the top of the screen was level with her eyes;
- an adjustable chair and footrest were provided;
- the employee was instructed in how to adjust her chair properly;
- the employee was supplied with a headset and instructed in its use which freed both hands for typing.

A month after the changes had been made the employee reported that her pains and discomfort had gone.

32   Sometimes it is necessary to provide personal protection (PPE) such as respirators, ear defenders and face visors, as well as other measures. For example a local ventilation system may be provided for pouring a hazardous chemical so that the operator does not breathe in the fumes. However, if the chemical can also cause skin burns, protective clothing, gloves and a visor may be needed.

33   Because PPE protects only the wearer, and only if properly worn all of the time, it is better to give priority to measures which protect numbers of employees rather than individuals. PPE can be expensive to buy and maintain. Employees will need to be trained and supervised so that it is properly worn at all times. The use of PPE at work is governed by the Personal Protective Equipment at Work Regulations 1992. If PPE is used in your workplace check the requirements of these Regulations. It should always be considered as a last not a first resort.

34   It is better to give those who have to wear personal protection a choice. Many companies make the mistake of requiring employees to wear it but give no choice about type, or fail to explain why it is necessary or to provide training in how it should be worn and periodically checked, cleaned and maintained. Not surprisingly, the use of personal protection stops fairly quickly. Managers can set a good example by wearing PPE themselves even though they might expect to be exposed for only a short time.

35   If you are thinking of moving to different premises or changing the layout of the workplace, this is an ideal time to think about risks to health (and safety), and make decisions about how to improve working conditions (Box 16 and 17).

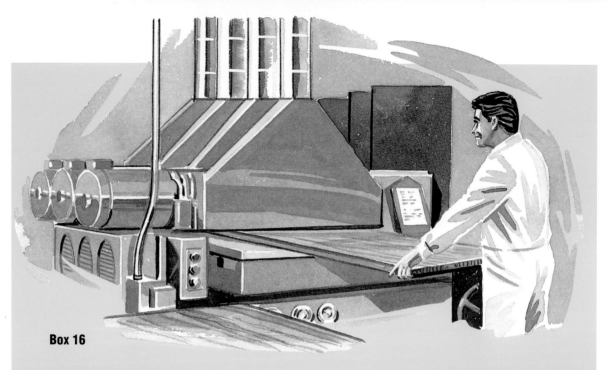

Box 16

A new management team at a factory manufacturing coffins decided that improvements were needed to working methods and efficiency. They reorganised the factory, resited machines, bought new ones and got rid of others. The machines were laid out according to the order of the process. Sanding was identified as particularly dusty and was relocated to a separate building and exhaust ventilation to capture dust was provided. The changes resulted in greater efficiency, improvements to both working conditions and health and safety.

Box 17

A company with 80 employees took the opportunity to improve working conditions when they moved to new premises. The company manufactured fibreglass products and handled harmful chemicals such as styrene. They were aware of the requirements of COSHH and also wished to be certified under the quality standard BSEN ISO 9002. Budgeting for health and safety was included in the costs for the move. Advice was sought from suppliers and consultants. As a consequence of the move, new plant was installed and new work practices introduced to control fumes, reduce waste and improve efficiency. Exposure to styrene was reduced by around 50%.

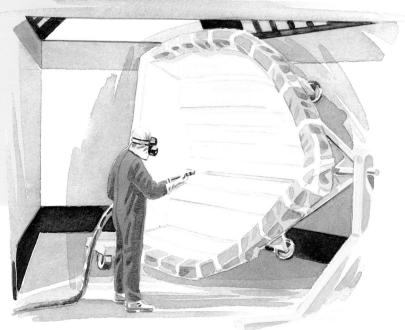

CHECKING WHAT YOU HAVE DONE

36   Once you have gone through the processes of deciding what to do and taking action, you need to check the result. There is little value in making changes without knowing if they are working.

37   There are a number of practical checks that you can make. These include checking that, for example:

   •   any set target for reducing health risks has been reached (Box 18);

Box 18

One company set itself a target of reducing noise levels over a period of two years. They wanted to reduce levels to below 90 dB(A) as required by the Noise at Work Regulations. Noise enclosures were fitted around noisy machines. The noise levels were then checked to see if the below 90 dB(A) target had been reached – it had. The workforce felt that management had demonstrated they were serious about improving working conditions. The workforce played a major part in the design and development of the noise enclosures.

- ventilation systems, noise enclosures, automated handling equipment are working properly (Box 19);

- records of sickness absence and work-related ill health show a reduced number of cases (Box 20);

- personal protection is being properly used, cleaned and maintained.

Box 19

A company installed ventilation equipment to control dust made during the weighing out of powdered chemicals. Air flow rates of the ventilation equipment and airborne levels of the chemicals handled were measured routinely. A fall in air flow rates or high levels of dust were used as a trigger for an investigation to find out why the control equipment was not working properly.

38   Remember that if for any reason you:

- make changes to the work process;

- introduce new materials into the workplace;

- change the way in which risks are controlled;

you will need to check whether these changes have reduced or increased risks to health. Do not assume that everyone will make changes and pick up new skills without instruction and training.

Box 20

An engineering company produced small assembly components. The production process consisted of repetitive operations with employees' hands and arms in awkward positions. Sickness absence and ill-health records showed a number of employees affected by upper limb disorders (ULD). Changes were made to the production process to reduce repetitive operations and to the layout of the work areas. A check on sickness absence and ill-health records showed that employees were taking less time off work with strain injuries.

CHECKLIST

FEEDBACK

Do noise levels, levels of airborne chemicals, performance of ventilation equipment and checks on housekeeping show that health risks are being controlled?

Do maintenance records show that controls such as noise enclosures and ventilating plant are being properly maintained?

Do maintenance records show that personal protective equipment such as respirators and hearing protection is being properly maintained?

Do records of sickness absence and ill health show an improvement?

39   Finally, remember that health risk management should be seen as a rolling programme of improvement. You may not be able to give satisfactory answers to all of the earlier questions or those in the following checklist. If this is the case, use this guidance to help identify exactly what priorities you set, decide how to do this and then do it. Then ask the same questions again to see how you have improved. It takes time and commitment, but you can improve and show to yourself that you have done so.

WHERE TO GO FOR HELP

40   You may well be able to solve your own problems but if you do need outside help there are various organisations to turn to such as trade associations, employers organisations, trade unions or your local Chamber of Commerce. The type of problem will indicate the nature of the specialist help you may need. Table 2 (p 38) has been drawn up to help you. Some organisations operate as consultants and specialise in particular aspects of work-related ill health. Others offer a wide range of services.

41   Use the free HSE leaflet *Selecting a health and safety consultancy* to help you choose the right consultancy for your needs.

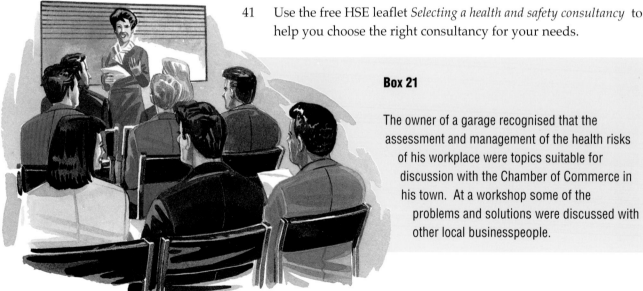

Box 21

The owner of a garage recognised that the assessment and management of the health risks of his workplace were topics suitable for discussion with the Chamber of Commerce in his town. At a workshop some of the problems and solutions were discussed with other local businesspeople.

42   Advice on the control of health risks at work can also be provided by HSE inspectors who can give advice on the prevention and control of risks and on legal requirements. The Employment Medical Advisory Service (EMAS) is a team of doctors and nurses who can advise on health problems arising from work and their prevention. They can also advise on fitness for work, first aid and the role of occupational health services. Details of HSE regional offices are given at the back of this guide.

43   If your business is an office, shop, warehouse, consumer service, restaurant, hotel, or leisure entertainment venue, you should contact your local authority whose address is in the telephone directory for advice.

Box 22

An engineering company knew from a survey of noise levels that they had a serious noise problem with machines used to chop up lengths of wire. The company sought advice from HSE who supplied a list of noise consultants.They selected a noise engineer who helped them design and make noise enclosures for the machines. They also measured the noise levels which were significantly reduced: the company considered the expenditure to be good value.

Table 2   **Occupational health specialists**

Specialists	Help they can give
Engineers	Ventilation engineers advise on the design and effectiveness of general and local exhaust ventilation to control exposure to airborne hazards to health such as mists, dusts, gases, vapours and fumes. Noise engineers advise on the cause and reduction of noise and vibration. Water treatment engineers advise on the design and treatment of water systems to avoid and control the risk of microbial contamination (eg Legionella).
Occupational hygienists	Assessment and practical advice on the prevention or reduction of risks to health from chemical, biological and physical agents arising from work activities.
Occupational health nurses	Assessment of risks to health; health surveillance; fitness for work; first aid.
Occupational health doctors	Diagnosis of work-related disease; assessment of risks to health and advice on managing those risks; health surveillance; fitness for work and rehabilitation; vaccination.

Ergonomists	Advice on: - the prevention of musculo-skeletal disorders, eg back injuries and upper limb disorders at work; - the suitability for use of equipment and workstations; - the physical work environment, eg lighting and temperature; - work organisation, eg machine paced work, as it affects health; - workplace, task and product design.
Radiation protection advisers	Advice on compliance with the Ionising Radiation Regulations; advice on monitoring, risk assessment and production methods; conducting environmental monitoring; some also advise on non-ionising radiation.
Non-ionising radiation	Specialist consultancies, university radiation protection officers and hospital physicists can be approached for advice on measures to prevent or control exposure.
Microbiologists	Assessment of biological agents likely to be present; advice on risk and control measures to prevent or control risks to health; sampling for micro-organisms.

Each of these groups has its own professional body who may be able to advise on selection and appropriate qualifications.

FINAL CHECKLIST

You have already been given some questions to help you spot hazards, assess risks and check what you have done.

You can also check how well you are managing work-related health risks overall by answering these questions:

Do directors and senior managers know what they want to achieve in relation to work-related health risks?

What priorities have been set?

Are those in the organisation responsible for work-related health risks aware of their responsibilities?

Is the role of in-house and external sources of expertise clear?

How are responsible directors, managers etc accountable?

Is there active involvement of employees, health and safety representatives and committee members, in-house and external specialists in spotting work-related health risks, making risk assessments and deciding on methods of control?

☐ Is everyone who needs to be, told about risks to their health at work?

☐ Are employees properly trained to:
- avoid risks to their health at work,
- make proper use of control measures,
- make proper use of PPE?

☐ Has a competent adviser been appointed?

☐ Are there any arrangements for monitoring exposure?

☐ Is there a plan to make progressive improvements?

☐ Are checks carried out on whether plans are being implemented and priorities being tackled?

☐ What are the arrangements for health surveillance?

☐ Is there a proper system for recording and analysing cases of work-related ill health and sickness absence?

☐ Are cases of ill health and sickness absence investigated so that lessons can be learnt and steps taken to prevent a similar problem arising again?

FURTHER READING

The following list of HSE publications is only a small selection of those available - a comprehensive list is available from HSE Books. Free leaflets are also available from HSE Books.

Managing health risks

Management of health and safety at work. The Management of Health and Safety at Work Regulations 1992 Approved Code of Practice L21 2000 ISBN 0 7176 2488 9

Successful health and safety and safety management HSG65(rev) 1997 ISBN 0 7176 1276 7

Essentials of health and safety at work 1994 ISBN 0 7176 0716 X

Managing health and safety: Five steps to success INDG275 1998 (free leaflet)

Guidance on the law

General COSHH ACOP and Carcinogens ACOP and Biological Agents ACOP. Control of Substances Hazardous to Health Regulations 1999 Approved Codes of Practice L5 1999 ISBN 0 7176 1670 3

Control of lead at work Approved Code of Practice COP 2(rev) 1998 ISBN 0 7176 1506 5

Work with Ionising radiation. Ionising Radiations Regulations 1989 Approved Code of Practice L121 2000 ISBN 0 7176 1746 7

The control of asbestos at work. Control of Asbestos at Work Regulations 1987 Approved Code of Practice L27 1999 ISBN 0 7176 1673 8

Introducing the Noise at Work Regulations: A brief guide to the requirements for controlling noise at work INDG75(rev) 1992 (single copies available free , multiple copies available in priced packs of 15, ISBN 0 7176 0961 8)

Manual handling. Manual Handling Operations Regulations 1992 Guidance on Regulations L23 1998 ISBN 0 7176 2415 3

Display screen equipment work. Health and Safety (Display Screen Equipment) Regulations 1992 Guidance on Regulations L26 1992 ISBN 0 7176 0410 1

Personal protective equipment at work. Personal Protective Equipment at Work Regulations 1992 Guidance on Regulations L25 1992 ISBN 0 7176 0415 2

A short guide to the Personal Protective Equipment at Work Regulations 1992 INDG174 1995 (single copies available free, multiple copies available in priced packs of 10, ISBN 0 7176 0889 1)

Approved guide to the classification and labelling of substances dangerous for supply L100 1999 ISBN 0 7176 1726 2

The prevention and control of legionellosis (including legionnaires' disease) Approved Code of Practice L8(rev) 1995 ISBN 0 7176 0732 1

Risk assessment

Five steps to risk assessment: A step by step guide to a safer and healthier workplace INDG163(rev1) 1998 (single copies available free, multiple copies available in priced packs of 10, ISBN 0 7176 1565 0)

Other general guidance

Occupational exposure limits EH40 (revised annually) 2000 ISBN 0 7176 1730 0

Health surveillance at work HSG61 1999 ISBN 0 7176 1705 X

Protecting your health at work INDG62 1996 (single copies available free, multiple copies available in priced packs of 10, ISBN 0 7176 1169 8)

Health surveillance under COSHH: Guidance for employers 1995 ISBN 0 7176 0491 8

RIDDOR explained HSE 31(rev1) 1999 (single copies available free, multiple copies available in priced packs of 10, ISBN 0 7176 2441 2)

First aid at work. The Health and Safety (First Aid) Regulations 1981 Approved Code of Practice and guidance L74 1997 ISBN 0 7176 1050 0

Guidance on particular hazards

Work related upper limb disorders: A guide to prevention HSG60 1990 ISBN 0 7176 0475 6

Manual handling: Solutions you can handle HSG115 1994 ISBN 0 7176 0693 7

A pain in your workplace? Ergonomic problems and solutions HSG121 1994 ISBN 0 7176 0668 6

Guidance on the Noise at Work Regulations 1989 L108 1998 ISBN 0 7176 1511 1

Vibration Solutions HSG170 1997 ISBN 0 7176 0954 5

Hand-arm vibration HSG88 1994 ISBN 0 7176 0743 7

Hand-arm vibration: Advice on vibration white finger for employees and the self-employed INDG126(rev1) 1998 (single copies available free, multiple copies available in priced packs, ISBN 0 7176 1554 5)

Health risks from hand-arm vibration INDG175(rev1) 1998 (single copies available free, multiple copies available in priced packs of 10, ISBN 0 7176 1553 7)

Respiratory protective equipment: A practical guide for users HSG53 1998 ISBN 0 7176 1537 5

Copies of videos, *A matter of life and breath: Occupational asthma - the causes, the effects and how to prevent it* and *Hard to Handle* (about hand-arm vibration), are available for purchase or for hire from HSE Videos, Dept HV, PO Box 35, Wetherby, West Yorkshire LS23 7EX (Tel: 0845 741 9411, Fax: 01937 541083)

Prevention of violence to staff in banks and building societies HSG100 1993 ISBN 0 7176 0683 X

New and expectent mothers at work: A guide for employers HSG122 1994 ISBN 0 7176 0826 3

Health aspects of job placement and rehabilitation: Advice to employers MS23 1989
ISBN 0 11 885419 4
Medical aspects of occupational skin disease MS24(rev) 1998 ISBN 0 7176 1545 6
Preventing violence to retail staff HSG133 1995 ISBN 0 7176 0891 3
Violence and aggression to staff in the health services 1997 ISBN 0 7176 1466 2
Passive smoking at work INDG63(rev1) (single copies available free, multiple copies available in priced packs of 10, ISBN 0 7176 0882 4)
Violence to staff INDG69(rev) 1996 (single copies available free, multiple copies available in priced packs of 10, ISBN 0 7176 1271 6)
What your doctor needs to know INDG116 1992 (free leaflet)

Harmful substances

Asbestos: Exposure limits and measurement of airborne dust concentrations EH10(rev) 1995
ISBN 0 7176 0907 3
Control of lead at work COP2 1998 ISBN 0 7176 1506 5
Provision, use and maintenance of hygiene facilities for work with asbestos insulation and coatings 1990
EH47(rev) ISBN 0 11 885567 0
In situ timber treatment using timber preservatives GS46 1989 ISBN 0 11 885413 5
Introduction to local exhaust ventilation HSG37 1993 ISBN 0 7176 1001 2
The maintenance, examination and testing of local exhaust ventilation HSG54 1990
ISBN 0 11 885438 0
The control of legionellosis including legionnaires' disease HSG70 1993 ISBN 0 7176 0451 9
COSHH and peripatetic workers HSG77 1992 ISBN 0 11 885733 9
A step by step guide to COSHH assessment HSG97 1993 ISBN 0 7176 1446 8

Seven steps to successful substitution of hazardous substances HSG110 1994 ISBN 0 7176 0695 3

CHIP 2 for everyone. Chemicals (Hazard Information and Packaging for Supply) Regulations 1994 HSG126 1995 ISBN 0 7176 0857 3

The safe use of pesticides for non-agricultural purposes Approved Code of Practice L9 1995 ISBN 0 7176 0542 6

A guide to the Asbestos (Licensing) Regulations 1983 L11 1999 ISBN 0 7176 2435 8

The control of asbestos at work. Control of Asbestos at Work Regulations 1987 Approved Code of Practice L27 1999 ISBN 0 7176 1673 8

Working with asbestos in buildings INDG289 1999 (single copies available free, multiple copies available in priced packs of 10, ISBN 0 7176 1697 5)

Work with asbestos insulation, asbestos coating and asbestos insulating board. Control of Asbestos at Work Regulations 1987 L28 1999 ISBN 0 7176 1674 6

Preventing asthma at work L55 1994 ISBN 0 7176 0661 9

Pesticides: Code of practice for the safe use of pesticides on farms and holdings (HSC/MAFF) (available from The Stationery Office, Publication Centre, Orders Dept, PO Box 276, London SW8 5DT Tel: 020 7873 9090) ISBN 0 11 242892 4

Breathe freely: A workers' information card on respiratory sensitisers INDG172 (available in packs of 25, ISBN 0 7176 0771 2)

COSHH: A brief guide for to the Regulations INDG136(rev1) 1999 (single copies available free, multiple copies available in priced packs of 10, ISBN 0 7176 2444 7)

Grain dust in non-agricultural workplaces INDG140 1993 (free leaflet)

Health surveillance programmes for employees exposed to metalworking fluids INDG165 1994 (free leaflet)

Health risks from metalworking fluids INDG167 1994 (free leaflet)

Management of metalworking fluids INDG168 1994 (free leaflet)

The complete idiot's guide to CHIP INDG181(rev1) 1999 (single copies available free, multiple copies available in priced packs of 5, ISBN 0 7176 2439 0)

Why do I need a safety data sheet? INDG182 1994 (single copies available free, multiple copies available in priced packs of 10, ISBN 0 7176 0895 6)

Read the label: How to find out if chemicals are dangerous INDG186 1995 (single copies available free, multiple copies available in priced packs of 10, ISBN 0 7176 0898 0)

Getting help

Need help on health and safety? INDG322 2000 (single copies available free, multiple copies available in priced packs, ISBN 0 7176 1790 4)

An introduction to the Employment Medical Advisory Service HSE5 (rev1) 2000

The future availability and accuracy of the references listed in this publication cannot be guaranteed.

The publications listed above may be obtained from:

HSE Books

PO Box 1999
Sudbury
Suffolk CO10 2WA
Tel: 01787 881165
Fax: 01787 313995

Alternatively, priced publications may be obtained from all good booksellers.

HSE REGIONAL OFFICES

London and South East
St Dunstan's House, 201-211 Borough High St SE1 1GZ

Home Counties
14 Cardiff Road, Luton, Beds LU1 1PP Telephone: 01582 444200

Midlands
McLaren Building, 35 Dale End, Birmingham B4 7NP Telephone: 0121 607 6200

Wales and West
Government Building, Phase 1, Ty Glas, Llanishen, Cardiff CF14 5SH Telephone: 01222 263000

Yorkshire and North East
Woodside House, 261 Low Lane, Horsforth, Leeds LS18 5TW Telephone: 0113 283 4200

North West
Quay House, Quay Street, Manchester M3 3JB Telephone: 0161 952 8200

Scotland
Belford House, 59 Belford Road, Edinburgh EH4 3UE Telephone: 0131 247 2000

Printed and published by the Health and Safety Executive   C10   8/00